Collectible Cats

AN IDENTIFICATION
&
VALUE GUIDE

by
Marbena "Jean" Fyke

COLLECTOR BOOKS
A Division of Schroeder Publishing Co., Inc.

D1307974

Searching For A Publisher?

We are always looking for knowledgeable people considered to be experts within their fields. If you feel that there is a real need for a book on your collectible subject and have a large comprehensive collection, contact Collector Books.

Photos by
Bob Fyke

Cover Design: Beth Summers
Book Design: Beth Ray

Additional copies of this book may be ordered from:

COLLECTOR BOOKS
P.O. Box 3009
Paducah, Kentucky 42002-3009

@$18.95. Add $2.00 for postage and handling.

Copyright: Marbena Jean Fyke, 1993
Prices Updated 1995

This book or any part thereof may not be reproduced without the written consent of the Author and Publisher.

Printed by IMAGE GRAPHICS, INC., Paducah, Kentucky

Table of Contents

Dedication

This book is dedicated to Tennessee and my family, without whose love, understanding and encouragement, this project would never have gotten wings and flown.

Special Thanks

Thanks to Tonya Fyke, Faith Carcone, Richard Ehelenberg, Dee Di Bello, and Maxine Roberts for allowing me to include special pieces of their collections.

Thank you to Lee Swartz, writer for *The Daze*, who gave me some background on black cat items.

A very special thank you to Sharon and Bob Huxford who gave me invaluable advice on photographing and who allowed me to be a general pest.

Last but not least a thanks to our able photographer's assistant Patti Fyke who gave us one of her few days off. We couldn't have done it without her!

Introduction

All cats, from the large jungle cats to the small house cats, belong to the cat family. Our domestic cats are the descendants of African wild cats.

The domestic cat has evolved as an urban scavenger and may have originated about 8000 BC, when nomadic humans settled into village life. From archaeological and anatomical evidence, however, it is impossible to distinguish wild from domestic types until the New Kingdom (1570-1085 BC) in Egypt.

The cat was then bred by a religious cult and worshiped as a sacred animal. Although the cat cult was spectacular, the cat may have been bred to rid Egyptians of the vast rodent population.

Egyptian cats were mummified and were given funerals as elaborate as the ones given for the pharaohs. They were given their own tombs and mummified mice were placed near them, so that they would have food in the next life.

Cat populations range from sparse to 2,000 per square mile, the largest being in urban areas. In some regions cats out number dogs.

Cats have been worshiped, condemned, and loved. Stories have been written about them, pictures have been painted and they have been immortalized in bronze, marble, and wood.

Cats played a roll in a battle between the Egyptians and the Persians. Their battle was not going well for the Persians. All seemed lost and the Persians withdrew and were missing for eight days. During that time they searched cities and towns, gathering up every cat they could find. When the battle resumed they released most of the cats onto the battlefield. Then each soldier carried a cat with him into battle. Not one Egyptian dared to harm the cats as that would have been sacrilege. Not one blow was exchanged and the Persians were victorious.

During the construction of the Grand Coulee Dam a cat played a very important role. The engineers had been unable to get a cable through a long winding pipe. A string was tied to the tail of a cat and the other end to the cable. The cat then went through the pipe and the problem was solved.

The breeds of cats are numerous, ranging from Abyssinian to Russian Blue. They can cost from $50.00 to $500.00 and sometimes even more. For myself, I prefer the plain old alley cat and especially a gray striper as they have the most wonderful dispositions. Of course as all we cat owners know, one doesn't own a cat, it owns you.

Cats are one of God's most fascinating creatures and this is why many people own them and collect cat objects. Cats rate #2 in the animal collecting field (dogs are #1).

In this price guide I have included a variety of cat collectibles and their current market values. My prices are based on my own personal experience in purchasing my collection at auction, privately and at shows. Prices vary from one part of the country to another. I hope this guide is helpful in your collecting endeavors and that you get as much joy out of collecting cats as I do. The field is endless and your next find is just around the corner. Good Luck!

Information Sources: Cat Catalog, Workman Publishing Co. NY pgs. 8 & 16. Prodigy (R) Interactive Personal Service, Academic American Encyclopedia, Grolier Electronic Pub. Inc.

A Bit About Collecting Cats

Collecting cat items can be an endless hobby.

When I first started, I decided to collect only black cats made by Shafford. Being the ardent cat lover that I am, this decision didn't hold for very long. I began to find a piece here and there and my collection grew by leaps and bounds.

Because the field is endless, one can specialize or collect everything in cat collectibles.

You should buy items that are in perfect condition, as they will retain their value. Of course, the older items are nice to have in your collection but there are numerous new cats on the market that can make welcome additions to any collection and become future heirlooms.

If you decide to collect only old pieces you should study antiques and collectibles a little so that you know what you are buying. There are numerous books on antiques and collectibles that list cat items. You will find them listed under each special category, I.E. Staffordshire, Doorstops, Black Cat, Banks, etc. Either buy a couple of good general books on antiques or go to your public library.

There are many reproductions on the market today. Iron doorstops, black cat items and glass cats are just some of the reproductions you will find.

Some of the newer collectibles of the future include Garfield and Kliban Cats. What's not to love about that fat cat named Garfield and there are an abundance of items to be found.

Kliban cats are the black & white striped cats with the red sneakers. They are not as plentiful as Garfield but items can be found. I even have a Kliban shower curtain, which is about ten years old.

Two other categories are glass cats and cat jewelry, especially pins. My collection of pins already numbers 142 and is still growing. There are some wonderful glass cats out there, old and new. Some are expensive but worth the price, as they should increase in value.

No matter which cats you decide to collect, there are cats in everyone's price range. The cost doesn't matter; it's the pure joy of collecting that counts.

Haunt the flea markets, garage sales and auctions. May you find the purrrrfect cat just around the next corner and enjoy collecting them as much as I do.

Black Cats

There are numerous black cat items but the original ones from the 1950's were made by the Shafford Company. The idea was conceived by Sanford Hartman in 1940. However, production did not start until 1950.

Shafford black cats were made of a red Rockingham clay. The first pieces made were two types of teapots. Each piece has red ears, a big red bow, green eyes and white whiskers and a high shiny glaze.

They were sold all over the country, from Robinsons in Los Angeles to Macy's in New York City. Other companies made look-a-likes, but Shafford cats out sold them all.

This is a partial list of items that were produced:

Ash Trays
Canisters (head only)
Cookie Jar (head only)
Coffee Pot
Cookie Jar (full figure)
Creamers & Sugars
Decanters w/Shot Glasses
Double Jam/Marmalade Pots
Utensil Holder

Wall Plaques
Egg Cups
Milk Pitcher
Mugs (two sizes)
Planters
Potholder Rack
Salt & Peppers (several types)
Spice Racks (6, 10, and 12 piece)
Teapots (5 sizes plus a double spouted one)

Some of the look-a-like companies were Wales Royal Sealy & The Royal Company of Boston.

There are a lot of other black cats to collect. The fascination with black cats stems from all the mystery surrounding them. In some countries black cats were thought to bring good luck, while in others they were believed to be evil and brought bad luck. We all know of course that any witch worth her salt owned a black cat. There is even a book on the market entitled *The Black Cat Made Me Buy It* by Alice L. Muncaster and Ellen Sawyer, Crown Publishers NY, copyright 1984. Black cats were used in advertisements for many years. What would Halloween be without a couple of black cats lingering around?

This category, alone, can keep you hunting for a long time.

Plate 1: Shafford 6-piece spice set, 9¼" tall x 7" wide. $125.00.

Plate 2: Shafford flat three-D ash tray, 2½" tall. $25.00. Shafford open mouth ash tray, 3½". $18.00.

Plate 3: Shafford stacking ash tray set, 6¾" long x 2½" tall. $45.00.

Plate 4: Shafford potholder rack, 5" tall x 4" wide. $85.00. Shafford letter holder, 7" tall x 5" wide. $20.00.

Plate 5: Three Shafford kitties, large 3½", small 1½". $15.00 set.

Plate 6: Shafford ball-type, 2-cup teapot, 5½" tall. $45.00.

Plate 7: Two Shafford mugs with original labels, large 4½" tall, small 3½" tall. $25.00 – 30.00 each.

Plate 8: Shafford jam & marmalade jar, 6½" long x 3½" tall. Note that lids have a J & M on them; each lid has an attached spoon. $50.00.

Plate 9: Shafford full-bodied creamer & sugar, 5½" x 4¾". $35.00 – 40.00 set.

Left–Plate 10: Shafford milk pitcher, 6" tall. $30.00.

Right–Plate 11: Shafford double spouted teapot, has two receptacles: one for tea and one for hot water. $65.00.

Plate 12: Shafford cookie jar, 6¼" tall. $85.00.

Plate 13: Pair of Shafford vinegar & oil cruets, 7½" tall. Note they are Mr & Mrs. He has "O" eyes and she has "V" eyes and a bow. $50.00 a pair.

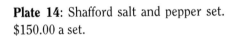

Plate 14: Shafford salt and pepper set. $150.00 a set.

Plate 15: One-cup teapot, 5½" tall, probably made by Wales Company. $20.00. Open mouth ash tray with gold eyes, 3½" tall, could be a Wales piece. $20.00 – 25.00.

Plate 16: Wales salt and pepper set with handles. $15.00 a pair.

Plate 17: Stack teapot set, maker unknown, in mint condition, made of red clay, 7½" tall. $65.00.

Plate 18: Large full-bodied teapot believed to be Wales, 8¼" tall. $30.00.

Plate 19: Figurine, 6" tall, rhinestone eyes, red clay, quite heavy, made to look like fur. $10.00.

Plate 22: Small Shafford figurine, 3¾" tall. $6.00. Companion piece is same size with yellow eyes, probably Wales. $15.00 a pair.

Plate 20: Figurine same size as plate 19 only smooth and not quite as heavy. $10.00.

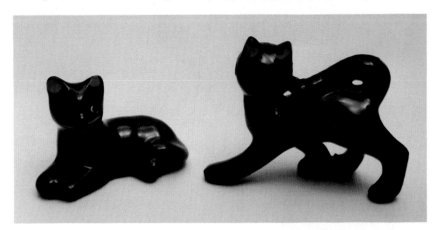

Plate 23: Two small kitties, by Wales 2", 2½". $10.00 a pair.

Plate 21: Toothpick holder, 2½" tall, could be Wales, red clay. $20.00.

Plate 24: Wales figurine, 6¼" x 4" tall. $15.00.

13

Plate 25: Cruet, 8" tall, maybe Wales. $25.00.

Plate 26: Black cat lamp, 9½" tall x 9", wide, maker unknown. $40.00.

Left–Plate 27: Decanter with cups, 11½" tall. I believe this is a Shafford set. Each cup has a cat's face painted on it. $55.00.

Right–Plate 28: Single bookend with pen holder, 5½" tall, maker unknown. $12.50. If anyone has the mate and would like to sell it I'm buying!

Plate 29: Small cat with goldfish in bowl, 3¼" x 3½". $10.00. This is a new piece but really charming.

Plate 30: Cast iron door knocker, 6½" tall, 1940's. (A little risque but nice.) $25.00.

Plate 31: Ceramic temple cat, 10½" tall, signed "M. Verne 1975." $15.00.

Plate 32: A crazy-looking sugar bowl has bristle whiskers and a metal nose, 1950's. $15.00.

Books

Plate 33: c.1901 book with illustrations by Raphael Tuck & Sons, designed in England, printed in Germany, 8" x 5¾". $20.00.

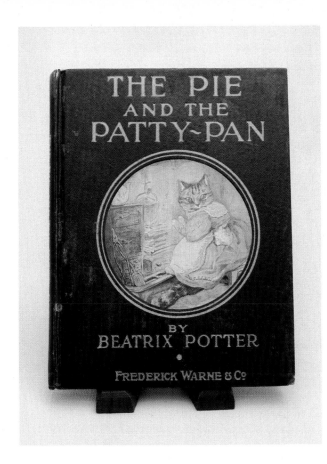

Plate 34: *The Pie and The Patty Pan* by Beatrix Potter, published by Frederick Warne & Company, 1905. Color illustrations and steel engravings, 7¼" x 5½". $20.00.

Plate 35: *Kitty Cucumber* by James E. Lillemore, published by Merrimack Publishing Corporation, 1983, Color illustrations, 6" x 4¼". $7.00.

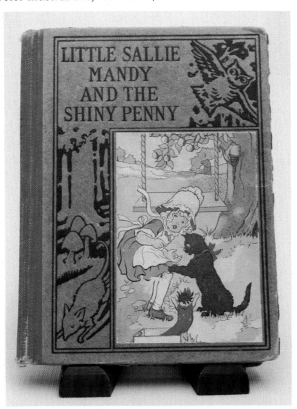

Plate 36: *Four Little Kittens*, published by Rand McNally & Company, copyright 1934. These illustrations are actual photos of cats and kittens. A note inside says that photos were taken with love and care not to harm the cats. This 1935 edition is $20.00.

Plate 37: *Little Sallie Mandy and The Shiny Penny*, by Helen R. Van Derveer, published by Henry Altemus Company, 1926, 5½" x 4½". $20.00.

Plate 38: *Cat's Revenge II: More Uses for Dead People,* by Hodge, published by Simon & Schuster, 1982. An answer to the one titled *101 Uses For A Dead Cat,* 8½" x 5". $10.00.

Plate 39: *The Black Cat,* a magazine published by The Shortstory Publishing Company, issued monthly, 1890's, 9" x 6". $15.00.

Danbury Mint Cats

Kittens Series, 1988. All are stone bisque with glass eyes and very well made.

Plate 40: "Sandy," 6½" tall. $75.00.

Plate 41: "Patches," 9" long. $75.00.

Plate 42: "Muffin," 7" tall. $75.00.

Plate 43: "Coco," 7½" long. $75.00.

Plate 44: "Pepper," 7½" long. $75.00.

Plate 45: "Snowball," 7½" long. $75.00.

Cats of Character Series, 1987. All are bone china. There were 12 cats in the series.

Plate 46: "Roly Poly," 5½" long. $15.00.

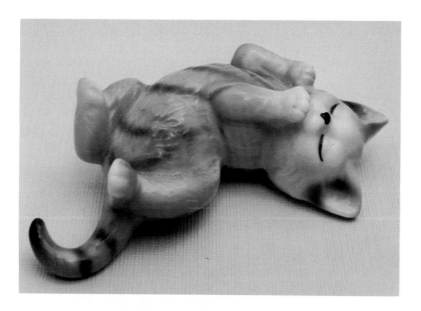

Plate 47: "Cat Nap," 4¾" long. $15.00.

Plate 48: "Bath Time," 3" tall. $15.00.

Plate 49: "Paws for Thought," 3½" long. $15.00.

Plate 50: "What's This," 3½" long. $15.00.

Plate 51: "Anyone for Tennis," 3¾" tall. $15.00.

Plate 52: "Stalking," 4½" long. $15.00.

Cute Cat Series, 1989. All are bisque.

Plate 53: "Inside Looking Out," 5" tall. "Easy Chair," 5½" tall. $29.00 each.

Plate 54: "Special Delivery," 4½" tall. "House Guests," 3¼" tall. $29.00 each.

Plate 55: "Hang in There," 4" tall. "On the Fence," 4" tall. $29.00 each.

Plate 56: "Grin & Bear It," 4" tall. "Goose," 2¾" tall. $29.00 each.

Plate 57: "Hide & Seek," 5¼" tall. "Mirror Mirror," 5¼" tall. $29.00 each.

Plate 58: "Suns Up," 6" tall. "Apples Away," 5¼" tall. $29.00 each.

Christmas Ornament Series. Twelve are shown here and the series is still in progress. Average height is 3".

Plate 59: Left, Mrs. Claus cat. Right, Little Drummer cat. $20.00 each.

Plate 60: Left, Santa Claus cat. Right, Candy Cane cat. $20.00 each.

Plate 61: Left, cat with goose. Right, cookie cat. $20.00 each.

Plate 62: Left, angel cat. Right, praying cat. $20.00 each.

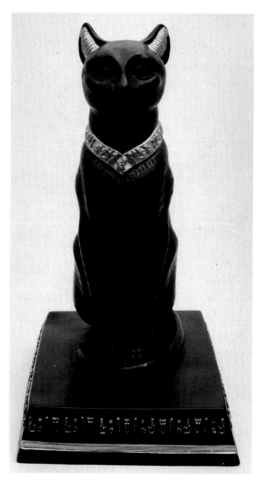

Plate 63: Left, gift cat. Center, skiing cat. Right, cat holding cat. $20.00 each.

Plate 64: Egyptian Temple cat, stoneware, 11½" tall x 5½" wide, 1989. $200.00.

Garfield

Garfield is the creation of cartoonist Jim Davis. He first saw the light of day in 1978 and has since graced the comic strips of 1,200 newspapers throughout the United States and overseas. He has also been reproduced in a series of books.

Although I don't believe that Garfield collectibles will appreciate much in value, he is certainly a fun addition to any collection. As I have said before, what's not to like about that fat and sometimes obnoxious cat.

Plate 65: Digital alarm clock. $30.00.

Plate 66: Telephone. His back is the entire phone and when you lift the receiver his eyes open. $60.00.

Plate 67: Lunch pail, new. $10.00.

Plate 68: Would you believe Garfield lunch bags? I have a package of 15. $2.99.

Plate 69: Wind-up. He dances around the floor, 1980. $7.00. Just a small paperweight, 1988. $6.00.

Plate 70: Bank, 3½" tall, 1987. $8.00. Christmas coffee mug, 4½" tall, 1987. $7.00.

Plate 71: Trophy 5". Mother's Day gift, 4". $5.00 each.

Plate 73: Pencil holder, plastic, 3½" tall, new. $4.00.

Plate 72: Bank, 6" tall. 1985. $10.00.

Plate 74: Two ceramic Christmas gifts, 4" tall. $5.00 each.

Plate 75: Ring or trinket dish, 3¼" x 2¾". $5.00.

Plate 76: Ring or trinket dish, 3¼" x 2¾". $5.00.

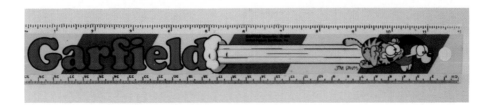

Plate 77: Ruler, new, 1988. $4.00.

Plate 78: Four coffee mugs that were McDonald's giveaways in 1991. $4.00 each.

Plate 79: Garfield cafe tumblers. $4.00 each.

Plate 80: Christmas ornament and can. I don't know what came in the can or how old it is. $4.00 each.

Plate 81: McDonald's Happy Meal giveaways, 1991. $2.00 each.

Plate 82: Plate, 8½" Danbury Mint Dear Diary Series, 1991, "I met a charming cat in the mirror this morning." $24.00.

Plate 83: Plate, 8½" Danbury Mint Dear Diary Series, 1991, "Today I found out why God created leaves." $24.00.

Plate 84: Plate 8½", Danbury Mint Dear Diary Series, 1991, "Tonight I thought I saw Uncle Ed in the fireplace." $24.00.

Plate 85: Plate 8½", Danbury Mint Dear Diary Series, 1991, "What a night! I had to do six encores at the club." $24.00.

Plate 86: Seated stuffed Garfield. This one is 3½" tall but the seated Garfields were made up to 15" high. $7.00.

Plate 87: Stuffed Garfield in a clown costume. Average height 8". $10.00-12.00.

Plate 88: Stuffed Garfield. Average height 8". $10.00-12.00.

Plate 89: Stuffed Garfield with a candy cane. Average height 8". $10.00-12.00.

Plate 90: Love Struck was on FTD Valentine arrangements in 1990. $10.00-12.00.

Plate 91: Stuffed Garfield dressed in an exercise outfit. Average height 8". $10.00-12.00.

Plate 93: Party gift Garfield, 4" tall. $6.00.

Plate 92: Stuffed Garfield dressed as Santa Claus. Average height 8". $10.00-12.00.

Plate 94: Glass Garfield bank, 7" tall. $15.00.

Glass Cats

Plate 95: Fenton glass "Alley Cat," 11" tall, 1970. $85.00.

Plate 96: Black glass paperweight, Langham Glass House, England, 4¾" long. $95.00.

Plate 97: Fenton glass cat, 3¾" tall, 1975 – 1990. $25.00.

Plate 98: Fenton glass cat, 3¾" tall, 1975 – 1990. $25.00.

Plate 99: Fenton glass cat, 3¾" tall, 1975 – 1990. $25.00.

Plate 100: Fenton glass cat, 3¾" tall, 1975 – 1990. $25.00.

Plate 101: Kerry glass cat from Ireland, 3½" tall x 1¼" wide, 1985. $65.00.

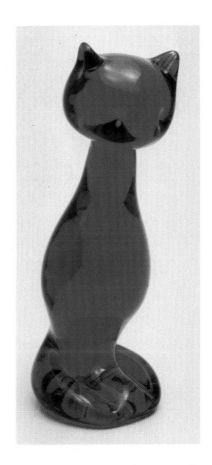

Plate 103: Red glass cat, 6½" tall, Viking, 1960. $35.00 – 50.00.

Plate 102: Glass wine decanter, 13" tall, 1950's. $25.00.

Plate 104: Round glass paperweight, signed "Joe St. Clair," 1985. $30.00.

Plate 105: Westmoreland dish, 5½" long, 1950's. $95.00.

Plate 107: Venetian glass cat, 9½" long, 1950's. $95.00.

Plate 106: Black glass cat, 6½" tall, 1985. $30.00.

Plate 108: Pilgrim glass cat from Massachusetts, 4" long, 1975. $15.00.

Plate 109: Fenton glass "Alley Cat," 11" tall, 1990. This was made exclusively for QVC shopping network and is part of the museum collection that was only sold on QVC and will not be offered in stores. $40.00.

Plate 111: Hand-blown glass perfume bottle, 3½" tall x 3" wide. 1940's. $25.00.

Plate 110: Venetian glass by Celleni, 11½" tall, 1950's. $165.00.

Plate 112: Boyd glass cat, 3¾" tall, 1980. $20.00.

Plate 113: Cobalt glass, 4" tall. $20.00.

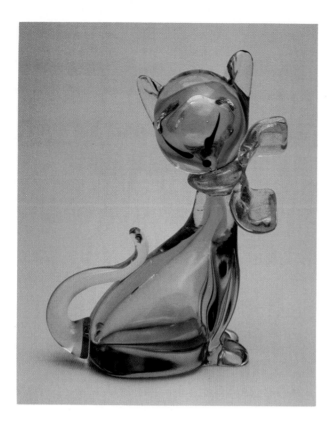

Plate 114: Venetian glass cat, 6" tall, 1950's. $90.00.

Plate 115: Satin glass perfume bottle, 6" tall, 1988. $18.00.

Plate 116: Westmoreland glass dish, 5½" long, 1950's. $90.00.

Plate 117: Westmoreland glass candy dish, glass eyes, 8" long, 1950's. $100.00.

Plate 119: Viking glass cat, 6¾" tall, 1975. $15.00.

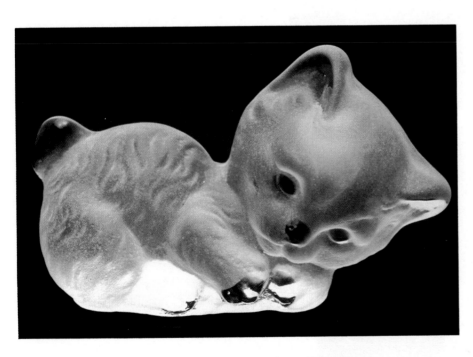

Plate 118: Viking glass cat, 5½" long, 1975. $15.00.

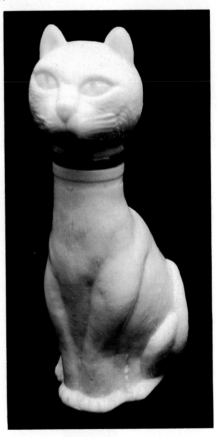

Plate 120: Milk glass wine bottle unopened, marked "Vintage 1971." $45.00.

Plate 121: New glass cats, maker unknown, 3½" tall. $15.00 each.

Plate 122: Swedish crystal cats, 1½" and 2½". $18.00 – 25.00.

Plate 123: Swedish cat, marked "NYBRO," 1980, 5¾" tall. $30.00. Crystal cat, 6½" tall, 1985 (companion piece to Plate 106). $25.00.

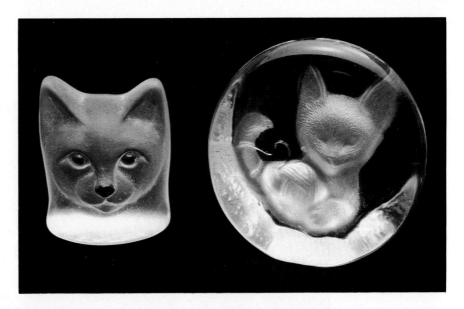

Plate 124: Glass paperweights: 2¾" tall, marked "NYBRO," Sweden $15.00 and 3¾" tall, marked "Zrgro." $15.00.

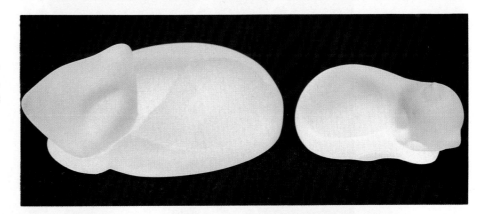

Plate 125: Sleeping cat, NYBRO Sweden, 1975, 4" long. $22.00. Sleeping cat, Franklin Mint, 1988, 2" long, part of the Curio Cat Collection. $22.00.

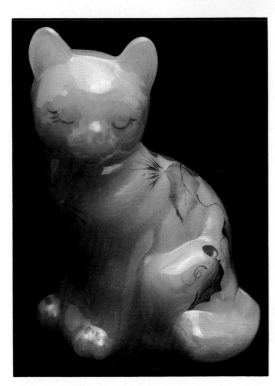

Plate 126: Fenton glass cat, 3¾" tall, 1990 Christmas cat. $25.00.

Plate 127: Princess House crystal cat, 4" tall, 1989. $20.00.

Jewelry

Plate 128: Sterling silver necklace, marked "Ole Calico Designs," 1978. This is a one-of-a-kind piece. The designer makes pieces to sell at cat shows and each piece is different. $140.00.

Plate 130: Sterling cat, hollow, 2" tall. $25.00.

Plate 129: Sterling silver cat on chain. The 2½" long cat is taken from an English teething ring and has a bell in it. $45.00.

Plate 131: Solid Sterling, 1 oz, Tiffany cat, ½" wide. $135.00.

Plate 132: Cat pendant from the 1950's, 3" long. $15.00.

Plate 133: Lion pendant from the 1950's, 2½" x 2½". $15.00.

Plate 134: New cat watch. $18.00.

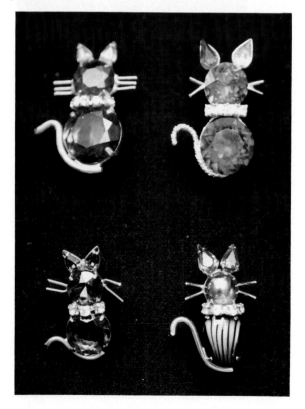

Plate 135: All of the pins above are from the 1950's. Top left $10.00, top right $12.00, bottom left $7.00, bottom right $12.00.

Plate 136: Cat pendant from 1950's, body of cat is hinged and it moves when you walk, 5" long. $20.00.

Plate 137: Three cat pins. Top, 1940's steel cut stones with spring tail. $15.00. Bottom left is 1950's. $9.00. Bottom right is new. $7.00.

Plate 138: All three pins are from the 1950's. $7.00 each.

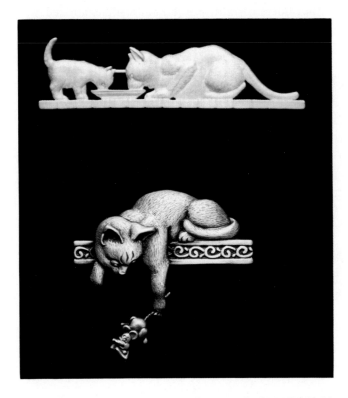

Plate 139: Both pins are new and are marked "J.J." $12.00 each.

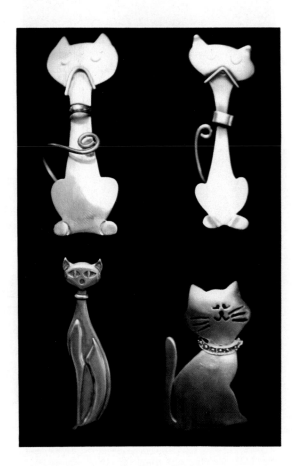

Plate 140: Top left, pin is handmade, sterling, 3" tall. $15.00. Top right, pin is handmade, sterling, and marked ORB. $18.00. Bottom left, sterling BEAU ART. $15.00. Bottom right, Pewter ULTRA CRAFT, new. $10.00.

Plate 141: Top, pin is handmade sterling 2½" long. $20.00. Bottom, pin is new. $15.00.

Plate 142: Top, sterling pin. $15.00. Center, sterling, handmade pin. $20.00. Bottom left, pins enameled. $22.00. Bottom right, pin is handmade enameled. $15.00.

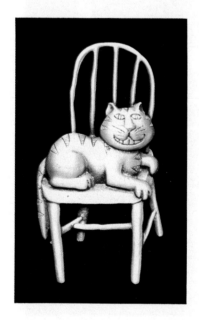

Plate 143: Pewter cat marked "J.J." $10.00.

Plate 144: All three pins are sterling. Left, Beau Art 1¾". $18.00. Center, handmade has Hallmark 1¾". $20.00. Right, handmade 2½". $18.00.

Plate 146: Top left, metal and turquoise, $7.00. Top center, enameled, $8.00. Top right, pink glass, $8.00. Center left, Marcasite, $9.00. Center right, Emmons. $12.00. Bottom left; ceramic, $8.00. Bottom right, rhinestone spring tail, $7.00.

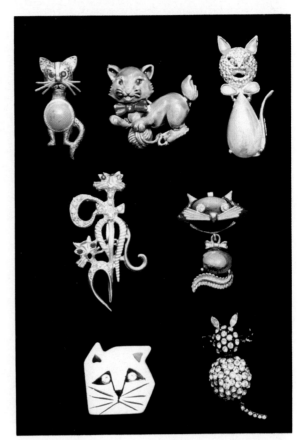

Plate 145: Handmade sterling cuff bracelet, 3" across x 1¼" wide. $30.00.

Plate 147: Top, Avon Christmas pin 1989. $6.00. Center left, cat pin made of fur. $5.00. Center right, cat pin made of wood. $4.00. Bottom left, 1940's enameled Fritz the Cat. $18.00. Bottom center, sterling with ruby eyes, marcasite and onyx 1½". $20.00. Bottom right, pewter 1¼". $12.00.

Plate 148: Top left, enameled, $5.00. Top center, mother-of-pearl, $5.00. Top right, rhinestone. $6.00. Center, all are enameled left $8.00, center $6.00, right $9.00. Bottom, all are enameled lapel buttons. $3.00 each.

Plate 149: Top left, hand-painted wood, $4.00. Top right, pewter, $7.00. Center left, bronzetone $6.00. Center, pewter, $7.00. Center right, heavy brass painted eyes, $6.00. Bottom, cat pin is handmade copper 2" tall. $15.00.

Plate 150: Top, both pins are hand-painted porcelain. Left $10.00, right $15.00. Center, made by the 1928 Jewelry Company, 3" tall. $18.00. Bottom, 2" wide x 2½" tall, new. $10.00.

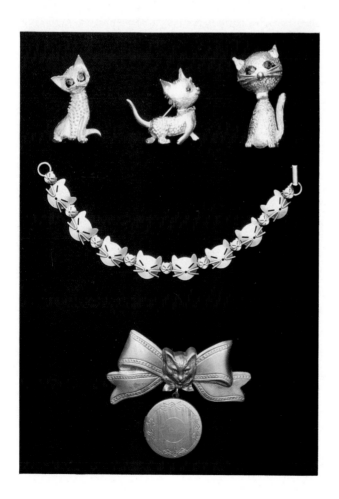

Plate 151: Top left, goldtone with rhinestone eyes, $6.00. Top center, goldtone with rhinestone eyes, $8.00. Top right, goldtone with rhinestone eyes, $9.00. Center, Beau Art sterling bracelet. $18.00. Bottom, 1928 Jewelry Company locket. $18.00.

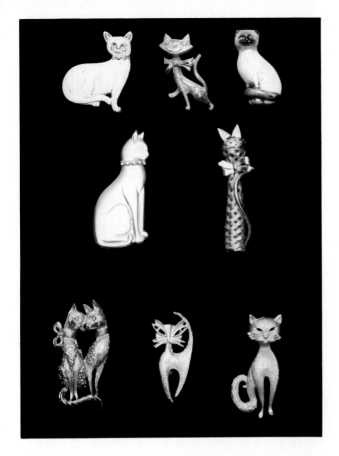

Plate 152: Top left, pin is enameled, $15.00. Top center, goldtone, $6.00. Top right, Avon ceramic, $7.00. Center left, brass and rhinestone, $6.00. Center right, brass and rhinestone, $15.00. Bottom left, goldtone, $12.00. Bottom center, goldtone, $6.00. Bottom right, marked "B & K." $7.00.

Plate 153: Top, 1950's enameled marked "J.J." $9.00 each. Center left, painted brass, $4.00. Center, goldtone/painted eyes, $9.00. Center right, has coral legs. $12.00. Bottom left, Avon. $7.00. Bottom center, head moves, marked "Jerry." $6.00. Bottom right, goldtone rhinestone eyes, $5.00.

Plate 154: Top, U. S. Postal Service stamp pins. $7.00 each. Center and bottom, Kliban enameled pins. $4.00-7.00.

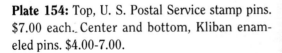

53

Metal and Wood

Plate 155: Pair of Egyptian Temple cat bookends, cast metal, 9½" tall, 1940's. $35.00.

Plate 156: Two small Chinese brass cats, 2" tall. $8.00 each.

Plate 157: Danish cat from the 1950's, 10" tall. $15.00.

Plate 158: Brass cat, new, 7" long. $10.00.

Plate 159: Wooden toothpick holder, 3¾" tall, 1940's. $20.00.

Plate 160: Hand-carved cat, folk art, dated 1976, 3" long. $20.00.

Plate 161: Paste brush with hand-carved head and glass eyes, 3½" tall, 1930. $25.00.

Plate 162: Hand-painted, hand-carved wooden cat from St. Martins in the Caribbean, 7" tall. $12.00.

Plate 163: Brass Tic-Tac-Toe set. Board is 6" square and cats and mice are 1½" to 2", 1987. $30.00.

Plate 164: Group of brass cats. Marked "China," large cat is 6½" tall. $15.00. Small cats are 1½". $8.00 each.

Plate 165: Handmade folk art fireplace match holder, 11¾" tall, 1940's. $18.00.

Plate 166: Pair of pewter cats with brass adornments, large cat is 6½" tall, small one 5" tall, 1950's. $70.00 a pair.

Plate 167: English bronze signed "Sue Maclaura," 5½" wide x 4" tall, 1920. $100.00.

Plate 168: Above, Russian nesting cats. Each one has 5 different cats. Ranging in size from 1" to 3½". $15.00 each.

Plate 170: Cast metal night light, 5" tall, 1940's. $35.00.

Plate 169: Hand-painted fireplace match holder, new, 8¼" tall. $10.00.

Plate 171: Cigarette holder and ash tray, cast metal in the manner of Frankart, 4¾" tall, 1940's. $45.00.

Plate 172: Oval brass box with pewter cat on lid, 5" tall, 1920. $50.00.

Plate 173: Round copper paperweight, 3½" across, 1950's. $22.00.

Plate 174: Handmade whistle, Russian, 6½" tall, 1970's. $20.00.

Plate 175: Left, Danish ballpoint pen, 7" tall, 1950's. $18.00 – 20.00. Right, Danish corkscrew and bottle opener, 7" tall, 1950's. $18.00 – 20.00.

Plate 176: Two hand-carved wooden cats, 6" tall, 1970's. $10.00 each.

60

Plate 177: Set of nesting boxes in the manner of Shaker boxes. Range 8" to 4½", 1970's. $35.00.

Plate 178: Pennsylvania Dutch wooden folk art cat, new, 6" long x 3½" tall. $10.00.

Plate 180: Hand-carved cat, 13" tall, 1970's. $25.00.

Plate 179: Cast iron doorstop, 9" tall, 1910. Paint is worn, $75.00 as is, $125.00 if perfect.

Plate 181: Cast iron doorstop, new, 8½" tall. $18.00.

Plate 183: Bronze cat on a marble base, titled "Golden Cat" signed Dewitt, 8½" tall, 1989. $135.00.

Plate 182: Hand-carved cat, 11¼" tall, 1980's. $15.00.

THE CATS' ACADEMY.

Plate 185: English pencil tin, 7" x 3", 1965. $15.00.

Plate 184: Cast iron lamp with Tiffany style shade, eyes light independently for a night light, 16½" tall, new. $125.00.

Plate 186: Droste Chocolate tin, 7" x 4½", 1920. $30.00.

Plate 188: Wooden cat hand-painted with oils, 4" tall, 1910. $40.00.

Plate 187: English chocolate tin, 4¾" x 4¾", 1965. $15.00.

Plate 189: Three hand-painted boxes, 2½" long, 1988. $10.00 each.

Salt and Pepper Shakers
and
Kitchen Items

Plate 190: Shawnee Puss-n-Boots creamer. $22.00 – 25.00.

Plate 191: Left, Danish Modern, wood, 1950's. $12.00. Right, ceramic. $10.00.

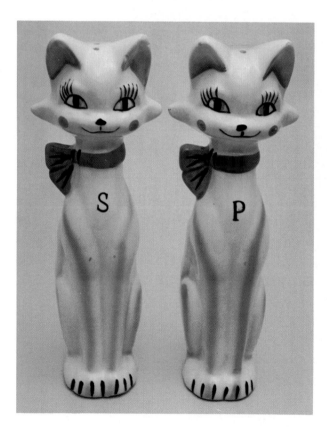

Plate 192: Ceramic tall boys. $15.00.

Plate 193: Salt and pepper shakers with toothpick holder. $15.00.

Plate 194: Both pairs are ceramic and well made. $15.00 each.

Plate 195: Pair of Indian kitties with napkin holder, made of bisque. $10.00.

Plate 196: Bisque salt and pepper shakers. $6.00. Ceramic salt and pepper shakers. $9.00.

Plate 197: Pearlized ceramic, probably 1950's. Left $12.00, Right $10.00.

Plate 198: Both pairs ceramic, fairly new, well done. Left $9.00, Right $8.00.

Plate 199: Left, wild deco cats. $12.00. Right, ceramic, they are magnetic (stick to each other) $10.00.

Plate 200: Left, ceramic, 1950's. $8.00. Right, ceramic, 1950's. $10.00.

Plate 208: Art Deco cats, $15.00.

Plate 209: Ceramic futuristic cats. $10.00.

Plate 210: Black cats, the pair on the left is old. $10.00. The pair on the right is newer. $8.00.

Plate 211: Left, meowers (shakers meow). $15.00. Right, ceramic. $7.00.

Plate 212: Left, shakers are ceramic, 1940's. $10.00. Right, shakers are stoneware. $7.00.

Plate 213: Left, shakers are bisque. $7.00. Right, Nodders 1930 – 40's. $25.00 – 30.00.

Plate 214: Left, shakers meow, ceramic. $15.00. Right, meows. $8.00.

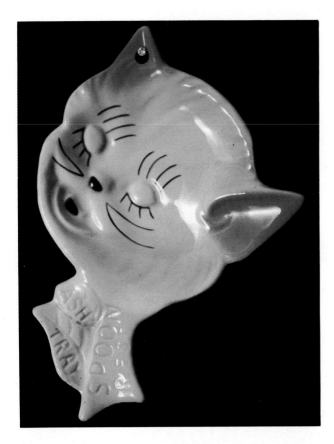

Plate 215: Ceramic spoon rest/ash tray, 1940's. $12.00 – 15.00.

Plate 216: Ceramic, napkin holder, 1940's. $25.00.

Plate 217: Set of ceramic napkin rings in rush holder, 1950's. $18.00 – 20.00.

Plate 218: Ceramic sugar bowl, 1950's, with original price tag from Montgomery Ward's. $15.00.

Plate 219: Cat butter dish, cat sits on fish base, 1950's. $12.00 – 15.00.

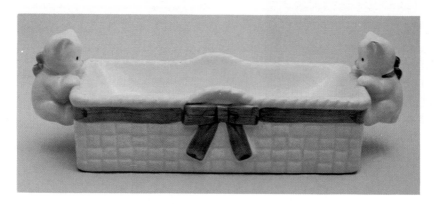

Plate 220: Cracker holder, 9½" long, 1975. $12.00.

Plate 221: Kliban cat coffee mug with one of the greatest cat sayings out of all my 20 coffee mugs. $10.00.

Plate 222: Wooden potholder rack with thermometer, 1940's. $20.00. Handmade potholders from 1950's. $10.00.

Plate 223: Handmade, hand-painted wooden matchbox holder, 1940's. $20.00 – 25.00.

Plate 224: Plaster of Paris kitchen reminder, 1940's. $15.00.

Plate 225: Black fat cat coffee mug, 3" tall, new. $5.00.

Plate 226: Czechoslovakian creamer, 1940's. $15.00.

Plate 227: Stoneware spoon holder, new. $5.00.

Plate 229: Lefton China creamer and sugar, 1950's, with original labels. $18.00 a pair.

Plate 228: Ceramic cookie jar, 13½" tall, no mark, came from California according to the dealer. I think it is very well done. $35.00 – 40.00.

Plate 230: Lefton China teapot, 1950's, with original label. $25.00.

Plate 231: Cream pitcher, impressed "N" in a circle, 4½" tall, 1940's. $12.00 – 15.00.

Plate 232: Avon creamer and sugar, new. $25.00.

Plate 233: Soap dispensers, 8¼" and 6½" tall, new. $5.00 each.

Plate 234: Ceramic teapot, 6" tall, 1988. $12.00.

Plate 235: Ceramic teapot with red fish spout, 5" tall, 1989. $12.00.

Plate 236: Black & white cat kitchen set, teapot is 8"
tall, cookie jar is 7½" tall, sponge holder is 3" long,
creamer and sugar are 3" and 4". $35.00 – 40.00.

Plate 237: Grey dressed kitty set consisting of cookie jar, utensil holder, sugar and creamer and salt and pepper shakers, new. $35.00.

Plates and Tiles

Plate 238: Bone china plate, no mark, 9½". $25.00.

Plate 239: Plate titled "Dominic" by Martin Leman, 9½",
1980. $25.00.

Plate 240: Bing & Grondahl Mother's Day plate, 6", 1971.
$28.00.

Plate 241: 6" Bone china plates marked Liverpool Pottery Ltd, England, 1956. $20.00 each.

Plate 242: Bradford Exchange plate, Velvet Paws Series, titled "Gymnastics," 9½", 1991. $35.00.

Plate 243: Bradford Exchange plate, Velvet Paws Series, titled "Playmates," 9½", 1991. $35.00.

Plate 244: "Three Kittens" milk glass plate from 1900. If perfect $35.00, as is $15.00.

Plate 245: Same as previous plate but painted to be a souvenir from Buffalo, New York, 1901. $25.00.

Plate 246: French Porcelain plates 4¼" called minou-ettes by C. Pradlie, not too old but very well done. $25.00 a pair.

Plate 247: Avon tiles made in 1991, artist is Mimi Vang Olsen. $20.00 each.

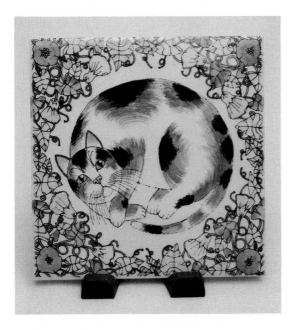

Plate 248: Above and right, three English tiles made in Leeds, England. I believe they are fairly new but very well done. $25.00 for the set.

Plate 249: Plaster wall tile. New but real cute and the saying is oh so true. $10.00.

Prints, Paintings and Photos

Included in this section are lithographs, chromos, steel engravings and prints. Chromos are lithographs in color and have a shiny surface. The ones shown here are Victorian although they are currently being reproduced.

Prices vary all over the country. I have based my values on my own personal experiences over the past twenty years and what I have paid and what I have seen them bring at shows and auctions. Prices shown are for mint condition unless otherwise indicated.

Plate 250: Victorian chromo of kittens playing with hat, 27" x 23" signed C. Reichert, 1893. $200.00 – 225.00.

Plate 251: Victorian chromo of kittens with bowl of cherries, titled "Three Little Rascals," 18½" x 23", 1898. $125.00.

Plate 252: Pastel signed A. Fletcher, 1973, 15¾" x 11". This artist has since died, a true loss of a talented man. $125.00.

Plate 253: Charcoal of siamese cat, picture is 10½" x 13" and frame is 21½" x 17½" signed Edith Alexander, 1946. $110.00 – 125.00.

Plate 254: Lithograph in the manner of Currier & Ives, 21½" x 15" titled "Puss In Boots," E.G. Ridout Co. NY/Caldwell Litho Co. NY, 1910, has some damage at edges main picture is o.k. $75.00.

Plate 255: Oil on Canvas, picture 12" x 8¾", frame 15" x 13", signed Balneba, 1920. $75.00 – 95.00.

Plate 256: Victorian chromo titled "Kittens at Play," signed Brand Neville, 25" x 23", 1910. $125.00 – 140.00.

Plate 257: Print titled "That's My Baby," picture 15" x 11½", frame 20" x 24", artist is Walter Chandora. I do not know the exact age of this but I believe it to be 1940's. $75.00.

Plate 258: Numbered print #4 of 25, artist James Boswell, 1952. $65.00 – 70.00

Plate 259: Steel engraving, 14" x 11", printing on bottom "Photogravure Goupil Cie," late 1890's. $50.00 – 65.00.

Plate 260: Victorian chromo of kittens in a basket. I have seen a postcard with this picture on it, 11" x 13", 1910. $65.00 – 70.00.

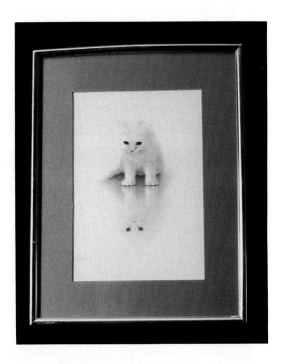

Plate 261: Print of kittens with spider titled "Distrust," signed L. Singer, 16½" x 13¼". $80.00 – 90.00.

Plate 262: Print of white kitten, signed but not legible, 1960's. $18.00.

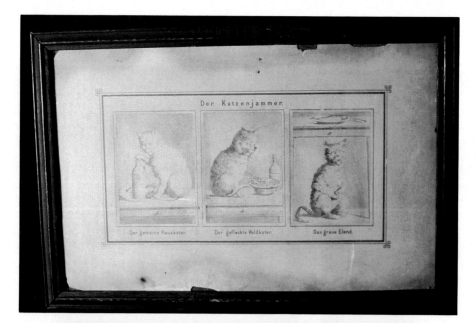

Plate 263: Early German cartoon photos titled "Der Katzenjammer," signed E. Binck, outside edge has some damage. $60.00.

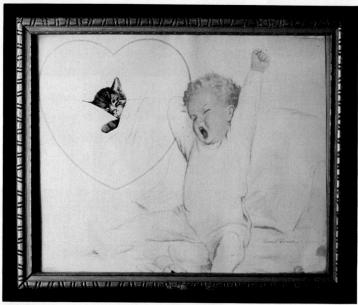

Plate 264: Print of Chessie, cat from Chesapeake Railroad ads, signed Lemuel Thomas, 7¾" x 9¾". $35.00.

Plate 265: Oil painting on wood, signed G. Worden, 10¾" x 8¾", 1953. $25.00.

Plate 266: Left, photograph of kitten in basket, 8¾" x 10¾", 1910. Right, photograph of kitten with vase, 8¾" x 10¾", 1910. These photos were also used on postcards in this time period. $35.00 each.

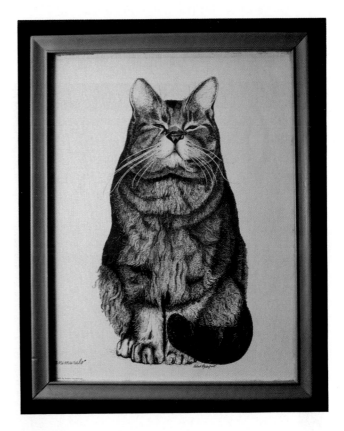

Plate 267: Print, signed but not legible from the frame. I judge it to be from the 1960's. Print 7" x 10", frame 15" x 12". $30.00.

Plate 268: Print called "Animural," signed Robert Leyderfrost, 12" x 15", 1950's. $65.00.

Plate 269: Oil Painting, signed M.C. Meirs, 18" x 13¾", 1949. This is a real folksy painting and is one of my favorites. $65.00.

Plate 270: Original charcoal titled "Winter Quarters," signed R. Snider, 15" x 16", 1920's. Matte is stained but I will not replace because of signature. $55.00-75.00.

Plate 271: Original pencil drawing titled "Who Are You," signed Luta Pluckman, 17¾" x 14¾". Matte has yellowed. $125.00.

Plate 272: Print of kitten in coffee pot, 8" x 10", 1972. $12.00 – 15.00.

Plate 273: 1940's puff pictures (kittens are raised), 6½" x 4¼". $15.00 each.

Plate 274: Litho of kitten between two puppies titled "Susie," copyright Daily Mirror Inc., 8¾" x 12¾", 1940. This print is easy to find. $12.00 – 18.00.

Plate 275: Print of Elizabethan cat made to look like an oil painting, print is 3½" x 4½", frame is 5" x 6½". I don't know the exact age of this but believe to be 1970's. $18.00.

Plate 276: Print of two kittens, signed Grace Lopez, 7" x 6", 1942. $12.00.

Plate 277: Poem with kittens looking at a fly, copyright Buzza-Craftacres MPLS USA, 5½" x 6½", 1950's. $15.00.

Plate 278: Victorian chromo of kitten with grasshopper, signed Varian, 7¼" x 9¼", 1910. $55.00-60.00.

Plate 279: 1896 calendar (foldout), calendar 2" x 1½" frame 5" x 4¼". $25.00.

Plate 280: This picture is included purely for sentimental reasons. All grandmothers will understand. My grandson was 4 and had 50¢ allowance when he was in a craft shop with his mom. He bought this sticker of a Victorian cat for me with his 50¢. My friend framed it for me and I cherish it. It is priceless to me.

Plate 281: Oil on wood, 4¾" x 3½". I don't know the age of it. It's been in my collection for 10 years. $40.00.

Plate 282: Watercolor, 7" x 7", signed AV, 1972. $50.00.

Plate 283: Round "Susie" picture with convex glass, 6" wide sticker on back *Harry Watson Studios, Hand Made.* $10.00-15.00. I apologize for the glare on Plates 281, 283, and 284. It is very hard to photograph these because of the convex glass.

Plate 284: Oil painting on what appears to be a heavy cardboard plate, signed but not legible, 10¾", 1890's. $85.00-95.00.

Plate 285: Two round prints, titled "Curiosity" and "Peace or War." These are both 6" in diameter and are from Harry Watson Studios. $10.00-15.00 each.

Miniatures and Smalls

Plate 286: Pewter kitten, 1". $6.00.

Plate 287: Three pewter cats average ¾" to 1". $8.00 – 10.00.

Plate 288: Pewter cats. Left, 1¼" long. $8.00. Right, 1¾" long. $10.00.

Plate 289: Two pencil sharpeners. Left, 1950's plastic TV, 1½" long, cat plays fiddle when you move it. $12.00. Right, chalkware 2" x 1½", 1940's. $15.00.

Plate 290: Left, flocked kitty with moveable paws, 1½", 1950's. $10.00. Right, bone china cat, 1½" long, German. $8.00.

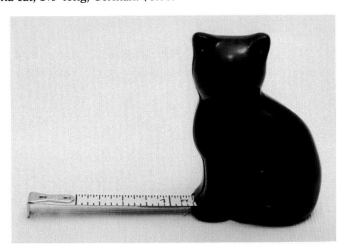

Plate 292: Tape measure, new, 2" tall. $10.00.

Plate 291: Beatrix Potter, Beswick, England "Tom Kitten," bone china. $30.00.

Plate 293: Beatrix Potter cats, Beswick, England bone china. Left, "Tabitha Twitchett," 1961. $35.00. Right, "Ribby," 1951. $35.00.

Plate 294: Left, Tabitha Twitchett & Miss Moppet, 1976. $35.00. Right, "Cousin Ribby," 1970. $35.00.

Plate 295: Harvey Knox Kingdom cat, bisque, 2½" tall, 1989. $15.00.

Plate 296: Left center and bottom, bone china bisque by Lefton China, 3½" long, 1960's. $10.00 each.

Plate 297: Lusterware toothpick holder, 2" long, 1940's. $20.00.

Plate 298: Occupied Japan celluloid cat, 2" long x 2¼" tall, 1940's. $25.00.

Plate 299: Goebel cat, Germany, 1½" long, 1970. $25.00.

Plate 300: Carved jade cat, 2" long x 1¼" tall, 1970. $30.00.

Plate 301: Franklin Mint Curio Cats "Bootscraper." $30.00.

Note: The Franklin Mint Curio Cats were first produced in 1989 and are being sold today. They do not seem to appreciate in value.

Plate 304: Franklin Mint Curio Cat, "Egyptian." $30.00.

Plate 302: Franklin Mint Curio Cats. Left, "Delft." $30.00. Right, "Satsuma."

Plate 303: Franklin Mint Curio Cats. Left, "Staffordshire." $30.00. Right, "Chalkware." $30.00.

Plate 305: Franklin Mint Curio Cat, "American Pewter." $30.00.

Plate 306: Franklin Mint Curio Cats. Left, "Ch'ing Dynasty." $30.00. Center, "Animalier," bronze. $30.00. Right, "Valencia." $30.00.

Plate 307: Franklin Mint Curio Cats. Left, "Cobalt" glass. $30.00. Right, "Netsuke." $30.00.

Plate 308: Franklin Mint Curio Cats. Left, Asian brass. $30.00. Right, art deco brass. $30.00.

Plate 309: Tidy Cat giveaways, plyable plastic, 2" tall, 1989. "Floyd" and "Tweeze." $5.00 each.

Plate 310: Tidy Cat giveaways, plyable plastic, 2" tall, 1989. Left, "Alex." Center, "Ruby." Right, "Rudy." $5.00 each.

Plate 311: Two Italian bisque cats, 2¾" tall, 1950's. $5.00 each. My son says the one with the red bow is a dog. I bought it as a cat. What do you think?

Plate 312: Pewter cat on Amethyst quartz crystal, 3¼" tall x 3" wide, new. $35.00.

Plate 313: Occupied Japan toothpick holder, 1½" tall, 1940's. $15.00.

Plate 314: Beatrix Potter Clip-on cat, "Tom Kitten," 3½" tall, new. $8.00.

Plate 315: Porcelain cat, 2½" long, no mark, 1950's. $10.00.

Plate 316: Left, cat on real yarn ball, 1½" tall, no mark, 1960's. $6.00. Right, Josef original 2" tall, 1950's. $7.00.

Plate 317: Bone china kittens in wicker basket, 1½" tall, new. $8.00.

Plate 318: Bone china cat, 3" long, no mark, 1960's. $7.00.

Plate 319: Carved composition cat in shoe, 3" long, no mark, new but very well done. $15.00.

Plate 320: Left, Bisque, 1½" tall, new. $5.00. Right, Bisque, Lefton china, 1¼". $7.00.

Plate 321: Left, bone china, no mark, 2¾" tall, new. $5.00. Right, ceramic, no mark, 2¾" tall, new. $6.00.

Plate 323: Carved wooden cat on silk pillow with wooden ball, not sure how old it is. Cat is 1¼" and pillow is 2" square. $20.00.

Plate 322: Left, Grey Goebel cat, German, 2½" tall. $15.00. Right, Carnival glass cat, could be Boyd not sure, 3" high. $15.00.

Plate 325: Bronze cat, no mark, 2" long, 1930's. $25.00.

Plate 324: Left, glass cat on stone, 2½" tall. $8.00. Right, Chalkware Halloween cat, 2¾" tall, 1940's. $18.00.

Plate 326: Cast iron cat, no mark, 2" long x ¼" tall, 1950's. $15.00.

Plate 327: Cast metal toothpick holder, missing some paint, 2" long x 1" tall, 1920. $20.00 as is, if perfect $50.00.

Plate 328: Two bone china cats, English, small ¾" long, large 1½" long. $20.00 a pair.

Plate 329: This the most unusual piece in my entire collection and nobody has been able to tell me what it is. The metal is pewter and as you can see it comes apart and the bottom is hollow. Could have held a thimble. The cat sits on what appears to be a champagne bucket, and is holding a fish in his paws. On one side it has KATER-STIFT and on the other it has a crest with two griffins. Between the griffins is a large "S" on top of a small "f." On the bottom are numbers and letters. It is definitely German and very old, I would say about 1900. It is hard to put a value on it but let's just say that I was offered $125.00 for it and didn't take it. 2" tall.

Plate 330: German bone china cats, 1¾" and 2" long. Left, $10.00. Right, 15.00.

Plate 331: Two Wade cats made in England, White Rose tea premiums, 1¾" tall. $5.00 each.

Plate 332: Carved ivory cat, 3¾" tall, 1920's. $30.00.

Plate 333: Left, stoneware cat, 1¾" wide, 1970's. $8.00. Thyssen Kermik cat from Denmark, 1½" tall, 1961. $25.00.

Plate 334: Left, German bisque, 2½" long, 1940. $10.00. Right, German bisque toothpick holder, 1¾" tall, 1930. $15.00.

Plate 335: Left, bone china musician, no mark, 2" tall, 1950's. $10.00. Right, bone china musician, German, 1½" tall, 1950's. $10.00.

Plate 336: Left, cast iron, 1" tall, 1940's. $12.00. Center, pewter cat, 1¾" tall, new. $7.00. Right, pewter cat on crystal cube, 1¾" tall, 1987. $15.00.

Plate 337: Left, Occupied Japan, ceramic cat, 2" tall. $10.00. Puss & Boots, Japan, 2¾" tall x 2¾" wide, 1940's. $15.00.

Plate 339: Left, carved jade cat, ¾" tall, 1970. $10.00. Right, plastic Argentina cat, 1½" tall. $4.00.

Plate 338: Left, German bisque cat, 2¼" tall, 1930's. $12.00. Right, Japanese bisque, 2" tall, 1940's. $7.00.

Plate 340: Left, German bisque, 1" long, 1930's. $8.00. Right, celluloid cat, 1" long, 1940's. $10.00.

Plate 341: Left, bisque cat, no mark, 2" tall. $5.00. Right, bone china cat, no mark. $8.00.

Plate 342: Left, copper cat with silver wash, 2½" long, 1950's. $15.00. Right, crochet cat, 1¾" long, 1956. $10.00.

Plate 345: Carved soapstone cat, 2" tall, 1920. $20.00.

Plate 343: Left, Occupied Japan. 2¾" long, 1940's. $10.00. Right, ceramic cat, Portugal, 1¾" tall. $5.00.

Plate 344: Left, stoneware cat with glass eyes, 3" tall, 1960's. $12.00. Right, stoneware cat, 1¾" tall, 1989. $5.00.

Plate 346: Stoneware kitty in basket, made in Scotland, 1¾" long. Left, $15.00. Right $7.00.

Plate 347: Two German bone china cats, 1½". $10.00 each.

Plate 349: Glass, 1" tall, 1950's. $10.00.

Plate 348: Just two cute cats no marks, 1" tall. $3.00.

Plate 350: Cast metal pin cushion, made in Italy, marked Frenzia. This is a nodder (his head moves up and down) 2¼" long, 1970. $15.00.

Plate 351: This is a "What's It." The cat is bone china, 1¾" tall, with holes for the spring to go through and a hook on the end. I have had it 10 years and I cannot put a price on it. (Thanks to Mrs. Innis of Washington state I now know that this is a teapot drip catcher.) $15.00.

Plate 352: Three plush kitties. The smallest is ½", the next is ¾" and the largest is 2". I believe they are from the 1950's. $15.00 for the three.

Plate 353: Left, ceramic cat, marked "N" in a circle, 2" tall. $7.00. Right, bone china, not marked, 1½" long. $6.00.

115

Plate 354: Two strange looking cats, no marks, one with gold accents but obviously made by the same people, 1950's. $10.00 a pair.

Plate 355: Left, Chinese cat, 1¾" long, 1920. $40.00. Right, tiffany ring box, 2" x 2", 1985. $75.00.

Plate 356: Left, Lefton china cat, bone china, 2½" tall. $10.00. Right, Lefton china cat, bisque, 3" tall. $10.00.

Plate 358: Three musicians, marked Dresden. These are pre-World War II. They are porcelain and 2¾" tall. $75.00 – 85.00 for the set.

Plate 357: Glass 2½" tall, 1950's. $15.00.

116

Miscellaneous

Plate 359: Cat seated on stoneware washstand with mirror, towel is like flocking, 6½" tall x 4" wide. $15.00 – 18.00.

Plate 361: Rubber cat toy with bell inside, 5½" long x 3" tall, 1940's. If perfect $15.00, as is $8.00.

Plate 360: Companion piece to plate 359. This one is bisque. $15.00.

Plate 362: Ceramic cat, marked artistic cats hand painted, 1990, 6½" tall. $7.00.

Plate 363: Ceramic cat, same as plate 362 only 9½" tall. $9.00.

Plate 364: Folk art cat, hand-painted stone, 6" across x 4" high, fairly new, very good painting. $10.00.

Plate 365: Musical trinket box, marked Westland, 3¼" wide. Lid is some sort of composition. $20.00.

Plate 366: Union Carbide giveaway plastic bank, 8" x 5", 1981. $20.00.

Plate 367: Russ handcrafted pottery fat cat, 3" tall, 1988. $15.00.

Plate 368: Stone bisque, new piece, 5" x 3¾". $8.00.

Plate 369: Lefton China, 5½" tall, 1980. $12.00.

Plate 370: Composition cat called a "Unicat," photos show front and back, 7" tall, 1988. $15.00.

Plate 372: Ceramic Satsuma-type cat, 7" long, 1986. $15.00.

Plate 371: Classic Critter sandstone kittens, 7" long x 4" tall, 1984. $18.00.

Plate 373: Minton bone china cat, 4½" long x 2½" tall, 1987. $50.00.

Plate 374: Royal Copenhagen cat, bone china, 4" long x 2¾" tall, 1976. $45.00.

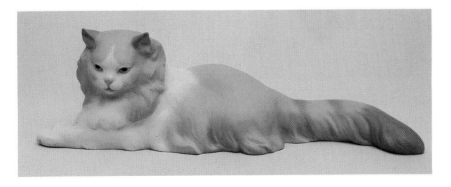

Plate 375: Bisque cat, 8½" long, fairly new. $25.00.

121

Plate 376: Ansley Cottage Garden, bone china ring dish, 4¾" long x 3" high. $25.00.

Plate 377: Royal Copley cat with original label, 7" tall x 5" wide, 1940's. $15.00.

Plate 378: Royal Copley cat with shoe planter, 9" tall x 8" wide, 1940's. $10.00.

Plate 379: Royal Copley cat planter, no label, 7" tall x 5" wide, 1940's. $12.00.

Plate 381: Small wooden puzzle, 7" tall x 5½" wide, about 1940. Did you ever try to photograph a puzzle? $15.00.

Plate 380: Royal Copley cat planter, 8" tall x 4" wide, 1940's. $12.00.

Plate 382: Large bisque kittens, no mark, 10" long x 6" high. $30.00.

Plate 383: Four Seasons musical cats with bisque heads and hands, 7" tall, 1987. $20.00 each.

124

Plate 384: Musical cat in basket, moves to music, 7" tall, 1990. $20.00.

Plate 385: Musical cat with fiddle, moves to the music, bisque head and hands, 11" tall, 1990. $25.00.

Plate 387: Shelf sitter, stone bisque, 5½" long, 1975. $18.00 – 20.00.

Plate 386: Two fishbowl hangers, Siamese is ceramic and 6½" long. $20.00. Little cat with fish is celluloid and 4" long. $22.00.

Plate 388: Jim Beam whiskey bottle, bone china, 11½", 1975. $20.00.

Plate 389: Garnier whiskey bottle, 9½" tall, 1956. $15.00.

Plate 390: Shelf sitter, stone bisque, 6" tall, 1977. $15.00.

Plate 391: Classic Critter, sandstone, 7" long x 5½" tall, 1988. $25.00.

Plate 392: Ceramic whiskey decanter, 10½" tall, 1950's. $15.00.

Plate 393: Chalkware cat with fishbowl marked Universal Statuary Co. I believe this to be a carnival prize. 9½" tall, 1948. $45.00 – 50.00.

Plate 394: Ceramic feeding dish, 9" long. $8.00.

Plate 396: Ceramic kittens in wicker chair, 7½" tall, 1987. $12.00.

Plate 395: Ceramic bank with lock, hand painted marked "Greatest," Japan, 7½" tall, 1940's. $30.00 – 35.00.

Plate 397: Ceramic clock, mark on face of clock "Tradition," 7" long x 6½" tall, 1950's. $35.00.

Plate 398: Sheffield ceramic clock, 10" tall x 5½" wide, 1950's. $60.00.

Plate 399: Ceramic cat, marked with "N" in a circle, 4" tall x 3½" tall, 1960's. $8.00.

Plate 400: Goebel cat, Germany, 4" tall, 1980. $20.00.

Plate 401: Left, Porcelain cat from Scotland, marked Highland Porcelain, 3" tall, 1988. $10.00. Right, bone china cat, German, 3½", 1950's. $8.00.

Plate 402: Papier-maché sachet box, 3¾" tall, not sure of age. $18.00.

Plate 404: Soapstone cat, 6½" long, 1985. $30.00.

Plate 403: Lefton China cat, 3½" tall, 1950's. $15.00.

Plate 405: Beyer's Choice Ltd. Christmas cats, chalkware, called "The Carolers," 3½" tall, 1990. $10.00 each.

Plate 406: Stone cat, 6½" long, marked "MT," 1971. $30.00.

Plate 407: Ceramic luster cats, 6" tall, no mark, 1950's. $15.00 – 18.00.

Plate 408: Musical cat, yarn ball moves with music, 5½" long, 1988. $15.00.

Plate 409: Musical stuffed kittens in wicker basket, Avon, 6½" long x 5½" tall, 1989. $20.00.

Plate 410: Siamese cats lamp, 13¾" tall x 8" wide, marked KROM, 1950's. $50.00.

Plate 411: Black cat wooden folk art lamp, signed Tony Amodio Maybrook NY, 1945, lamp base is 11" tall. $40.00. Flocked lamp shade is 1940's. Shade only $15.00.

Plate 412: Cast metal lamp in the manner of Frankart, 8½" tall, 1930's. $45.00. Lamp shade is part of a set of three (one is on the lamp in plate 411). I purchased them at a garage sale in 1980. They were in the original cellophane and had price tags of 49¢ each from F.W. Woolworths. I found the lamps 2 years later and the shades matched perfectly. Shade only $15.00.

Plate 413: Elizabeth Arden ring dish, made in France, 3" wide, 1979. $15.00.

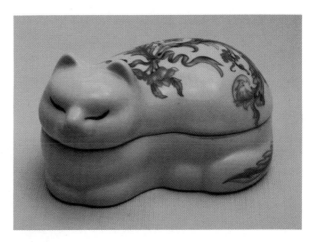

Plate 414: Elizabeth Arden ring dish, made in France, 4" long, 1974. $15.00.

Plate 415: Elizabeth Arden ring dish, in the manner of Satsuma, made in Japan, 5" long, 1990. $15.00.

Plate 416: Satsuma cat, marked Japan in red, 6½" long, 1920. $55.00.

Plate 417: Satsuma cat, marked with impressed Japanese characters, 4" long, 1910. $60.00.

Plate 418: Old Steiff cat, a bit of the fur is thin, 5" long x 2½" tall, 1945-54. $40.00 as is, $65.00 if perfect.

Plate 419: Tin wind-up toy, celluloid head and tail, 5" long, late 1940's. $35.00.

Plate 420: Tin wind-up toy, celluloid head and tail, 5" long, late 1940's. $35.00.

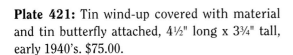

Plate 421: Tin wind-up covered with material and tin butterfly attached, 4½" long x 3¾" tall, early 1940's. $75.00.

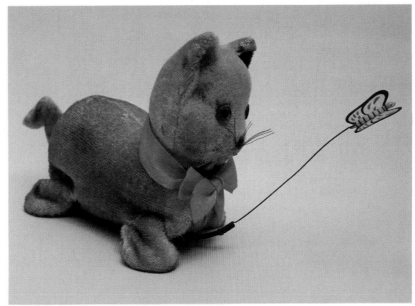

Plate 422: Tin wind-up covered with material, celluloid ball, 6" long x 3¾" tall, early 1940's. $70.00 – 75.00.

Plate 423: Papier-maché box, hand painted, 3½" long x 2" wide, 1950's. $20.00.

Plate 424: Plastic toy warbling whistle, 7" long, 1940's. When you pull the red ring and blow in it the bird moves and it warbles. $30.00.

Plate 425: Two 4" tall fairings from England. These were sold at country fairs. When you first look at them you think they are alike, but when you look closer you can see differences. $65.00 each.

Plate 426: Pair of cats in valises. No marks, probably Japanese, 1950's. $15.00 a pair.

Plate 427: Bone china cat with crown mark, 4" long x 3½" tall, German, 1910. $30.00.

Plate 428: Above and right, DeVilbis perfume bottle, made by Lenox China, 3¾"
tall, 1956. $65.00 – 75.00.

Plate 429: Two ball players, marked "Napco" (probably Japanese). $10.00 pair.

Plate 430: Staffordshire cottage cat, 3¾" tall x
2" wide. $60.00.

137

Plate 431: Harlequin cat, missing some gold, one of the mavericks. $20.00 as is, $35.00 if perfect.

Plate 432: Steiff excelsior stuffed cat, 3½" wide x 2½" tall has little brass bell, 1954. $40.00.

Plate 433: Stoneware cat, 4½" tall, no mark, 1950's. $10.00.

Plate 434: Bone china nodder, Lefton China, Japan, 4¼" long x 2¾" tall, 1950's. $15.00.

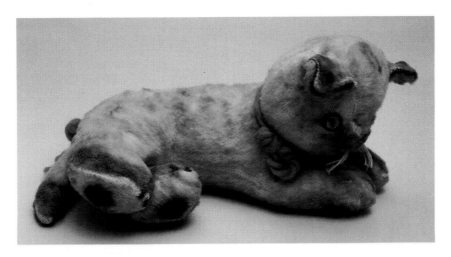

Plate 435: Old stuffed kitty with blue glass eyes, yarn on neck is not original. Probably late 1940's. $15.00.

Plate 436: Original "Skeeter Design," made of rabbit with blue glass eyes. This is a one of a kind. 8½" long, 1974. $25.00.

Plate 437: Steiff cat, green eyes, 6½" long, 1974. $40.00 – 55.00.

Plate 438: Cat, similar to Steiff, no tag, 7" long, 1950's. $10.00.

Plate 439: Cat treat jar, I keep my cat's catnip in it, 7" long x 5" tall, new. $15.00.

Plate 440: Stone bisque group, 4¼" long x 3½" tall, new. $10.00.

Plate 441: Creamware planter, no mark, 5" long x 3¾" tall, believed to be 1940's. $25.00.

Plate 442: Porcelain wall pocket, hand painted, luster ware, Japan, 6½", 1940's. $30.00 – 35.00.

Plate 443: Old bisque cat, no mark, believed to be 1920's, little damage on ear. $20.00.

Plate 444: Bisque cat, signed "Andrea" by Sadek, 5½" long x 4½" tall, 1987. $15.00.

Plate 445: The bottom part is half of a perfume bottle which is featured in the glass section, it was simply used to show this old pewter stopper, 1½" tall, believed to be early 1900. $20.00 – 25.00.

Plate 446: Molded plastic with mixture of small quarry stones inside, has moveable plastic eyes, 4" tall. I don't know how old it is or where it was made but it is really an interesting piece. $15.00.

Plate 447: Lefton China stone bisque cat, 6" tall, 1975. $20.00.

Plate 448: Handmade patchwork cat, very well done, 8½" tall, new. $15.00.

Plate 449: Molded plaster cat with material covered with polyurethane, 7" long x 3" high, new. $15.00.

Plate 450: Porcelain, 7" long x 4" tall, new. $12.00.

Plate 451: Set of Tennessee Folk art cats. These are covered with patchwork squares and covered with shellac. They have store bought eyelashes and whiskers. I'm not sure of their age. Big one is 10½" long x 7" tall. Small one 6" x 4". $35.00 a set.

Plate 452: Hand-painted porcelain cat, no mark, 7" tall, new. $15.00.

Plate 453: Card holder with place for pen, marked Takahasi Japan, crazed from age, 1950's. $15.00.

Plate 454: Stone sculpture titled "Wash Day," 4" tall, 1982. $15.00.

Plate 455: Bisque cats with top hat no mark, 4" x 3". $10.00.

Plate 456: Beswick cat, made in England, bone china, 6½" tall, 1950's. $20.00.

Plate 457: Stone sculpture titled "Cellini," this could be a makers since it looks more like it should be called "Spilt Milk," 1982. $15.00.

Plate 458: Goebel cat, made in Germany, 5½" tall, 1965. $20.00.

Plate 459: Lefton China bisque cat with red bow, 6" tall, 1950's. $20.00.

Plate 460: Bisque cat music box, rotates with music, marked Mann Japan, 4" long, new. $15.00.

Plate 462: Kliban cat in the hat, made of porcelain, 7¾" tall, 1979. $30.00.

Plate 461: Bisque cat in barrel, 6½" tall, 1988. $10.00.

Plate 463: Kliban cat with red sneakers bank, 6½" long, 1979. $30.00.

Plate 464: Ceramic ash tray, marked Mann, 8¾" long, 1970. $10.00.

Plate 465: German bisque cat, 5" tall, 2¾" wide, 1910. $30.00.

Plate 466: Ceramic Christmas cat, not marked, 10" tall, 1985. $15.00.

Plate 467: Left, ceramic cat no marks, 5" tall, 1950's. $12.00. Right, ceramic cat no marks, 4¾" tall, 1950's. $10.00.

Plate 468: Pair of porcelain dolls, 13" tall, 1970's. $45.00 a pair.

Plate 469: Ceramic bath salts bottle, 6½" tall, from the 1940's. Bath salts are still in it and have caused the black paint to bleed. It has a label but I'm unable to read it as it is worn. $25.00.

Plate 470: Parian cat made in Germany in late 1850's, mold numbers on bottom 59/3611, slight damage at top. This is the oldest piece in the book. $110.00.

Plate 471: German porcelain piece, 5½" tall. Early 1900's. $40.00.

Plate 472: Royal Doulton Flambe cat, bone china, 5" tall x 2½" wide. $165.00.

Plate 473: Celluloid cat, 6½" long x 4½" tall, 1930's. $50.00.

151

Plate 474: Flocked nodder with blue glass eyes, 6" long x 4½" tall, 1940's. $25.00.

Plate 475: German bisque vase with faces of a cat, dog and owl, 4" tall, 1920. $30.00.

Plate 476: Wade bone china cat made in England marked "SI." He is the Siamese cat from the Disney movie "Lady and the Tramp." $35.00.

Plate 478: Flocked nodders in wicker basket, have blue glass eyes, 1940's. $40.00.

Plate 477: Lefton china porcelain cat, 7" tall, 1960's. $15.00.

Plate 479: Avon perfume. $4.00.

Plate 480: Left, Avon cream sachet kitten on amber basket. $3.00. Right, Avon cream sachet called "Sitting Pretty," 1950's. $15.00.

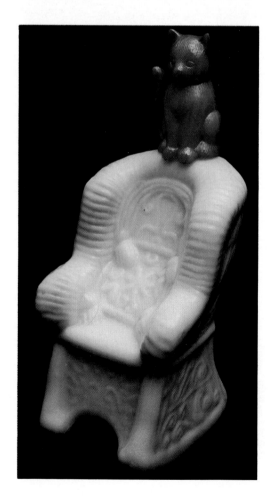

Plate 481: Avon kitten on rocking chair. $5.00.

Plate 482: Avon Ming cat perfume. $6.00.

Plate 483: Left, Avon white kitten on pillow sachet jar. $4.00. Right, Avon white cat perfume. $4.00.

Plate 484: Porcelain sculptured cat, bone china, English, 4" wide, 1965. $15.00.

Plate 485: Left, Avon black cat perfume. $4.00. Right, Avon white cat with ball of yarn. $4.00.

Plate 486: Porcelain sculptured cat, bone china, English, 4" wide, 1965. $15.00.

Plate 487: Bisque music box, marked Mann Japan, 6½" tall, 1988. $15.00.

Plate 488: Beswick England Cat. 7" tall. $1956. $35.00.

156

Plate 489: Beswick, England cat, 6½" tall, 1956. $35.00.

Plate 490: Sculpted bone china cat, no mark, 6" long x 4" wide, 1970's. $15.00.

Plate 491: Porcelain cat, no mark, well done, 1965. 7½" tall. $18.00.

Plate 492: White ceramic cat with green glass eyes, 8" wide x 7" tall, not sure of age, probably 1980's. $15.00.

Plate 493: Porcelain cat, no mark, very well done, 7½" tall, 1965. $15.00.

Books on Antiques and Collectibles

This is only a partial listing of the books on antiques that are available from Collector Books. All books are well illustrated and contain current values. Most of the following books are available from your local book seller, antique dealer, or public library. If you are unable to locate certain titles in your area, you may order by mail from COLLECTOR BOOKS, P.O. Box 3009, Paducah, KY 42002-3009. Customers with Visa or MasterCard may phone in orders from 8:00–4:00 CST, Monday–Friday, Toll Free 1-800-626-5420. Add $2.00 for postage for the first book ordered and $0.30 for each additional book. Include item number, title, and price when ordering. Allow 14 to 21 days for delivery.

BOOKS ON GLASS AND POTTERY

1810	American Art Glass, Shuman	$29.95
1312	Blue & White Stoneware, McNerney	$9.95
1959	Blue Willow, 2nd Ed., Gaston	$14.95
3719	Coll. Glassware from the 40's, 50's, 60's, 2nd Ed., Florence	$19.95
3816	Collectible Vernon Kilns, Nelson	$24.95
3311	Collecting Yellow Ware – Id. & Value Gd., McAllister	$16.95
1373	Collector's Ency. of American Dinnerware, Cunningham	$24.95
3815	Coll. Ency. of Blue Ridge Dinnerware, Newbound	$19.95
2272	Collector's Ency. of California Pottery, Chipman	$24.95
3811	Collector's Ency. of Colorado Pottery, Carlton	$24.95
3312	Collector's Ency. of Children's Dishes, Whitmyer	$19.95
2133	Collector's Ency. of Cookie Jars, Roerig	$24.95
3723	Coll. Ency. of Cookie Jars-Volume II, Roerig	$24.95
3724	Collector's Ency. of Depression Glass, 11th Ed., Florence	$19.95
2209	Collector's Ency. of Fiesta, 7th Ed., Huxford	$19.95
1439	Collector's Ency. of Flow Blue China, Gaston	$19.95
3812	Coll. Ency. of Flow Blue China, 2nd Ed., Gaston	$24.95
3813	Collector's Ency. of Hall China, 2nd Ed., Whitmyer	$24.95
2334	Collector's Ency. of Majolica Pottery, Katz-Marks	$19.95
1358	Collector's Ency. of McCoy Pottery, Huxford	$19.95
3313	Collector's Ency. of Niloak, Gifford	$19.95
3837	Collector's Ency. of Nippon Porcelain I, Van Patten	$24.95
2089	Collector's Ency. of Nippon Porcelain II, Van Patten	$24.95
1665	Collector's Ency. of Nippon Porcelain III, Van Patten	$24.95
1447	Collector's Ency. of Noritake, 1st Series, Van Patten	$19.95
1034	Collector's Ency. of Roseville Pottery, Huxford	$19.95
1035	Collector's Ency. of Roseville Pottery, 2nd Ed., Huxford	$19.95
3314	Collector's Ency. of Van Briggle Art Pottery, Sasicki	$24.95
3433	Collector's Guide To Harker Pottery - U.S.A., Colbert	$17.95
2339	Collector's Guide to Shawnee Pottery, Vanderbilt	$19.95
1425	Cookie Jars, Westfall	$9.95
3440	Cookie Jars, Book II, Westfall	$19.95
2275	Czechoslovakian Glass & Collectibles, Barta	$16.95
3882	Elegant Glassware of the Depression Era, 6th Ed., Florence	$19.95
3725	Fostoria - Pressed, Blown & Hand Molded Shapes, Kerr	$24.95
3883	Fostoria Stemware - The Crystal for America, Long	$24.95
3886	Kitchen Glassware of the Depression Years, 5th Ed., Florence	$19.95
3889	Pocket Guide to Depression Glass, 9th Ed., Florence	$9.95
3825	Puritan Pottery, Morris	$24.95
1670	Red Wing Collectibles, DePasquale	$9.95
1440	Red Wing Stoneware, DePasquale	$9.95
1958	So. Potteries Blue Ridge Dinnerware, 3rd Ed., Newbound	$14.95
3739	Standard Carnival Glass, 4th Ed., Edwards	$24.95
3327	Watt Pottery – Identification & Value Guide, Morris	$19.95
2224	World of Salt Shakers, 2nd Ed., Lechner	$24.95

BOOKS ON DOLLS & TOYS

2079	Barbie Fashion, Vol. 1, 1959-1967, Eames	$24.95
3310	Black Dolls – 1820 - 1991 - Id. & Value Guide, Perkins	$17.95
3810	Chatty Cathy Dolls, Lewis	$15.95
1529	Collector's Ency. of Barbie Dolls, DeWein	$19.95
2338	Collector's Ency. of Disneyana, Longest & Stern	$24.95
3727	Coll. Guide to Ideal Dolls, Izen	$18.95
3822	Madame Alexander Price Guide #19, Smith	$9.95
3732	Matchbox Toys, 1948 to 1993, Johnson	$18.95

3733	Modern Collector's Dolls, 6th series, Smith	$24.95
1540	Modern Toys, 1930 - 1980, Baker	$19.95
3824	Patricia Smith's Doll Values – Antique to Modern, 10th ed.	$12.95
3826	Story of Barbie, Westenhouser, No Values	$19.95
2028	Toys, Antique & Collectible, Longest	$14.95
1808	Wonder of Barbie, Manos	$9.95
1430	World of Barbie Dolls, Manos	$9.95

OTHER COLLECTIBLES

1457	American Oak Furniture, McNerney	$9.95
3716	American Oak Furniture, Book II, McNerney	$12.95
2333	Antique & Collectible Marbles, 3rd Ed., Grist	$9.95
1748	Antique Purses, Holiner	$19.95
1426	Arrowheads & Projectile Points, Hothem	$7.95
1278	Art Nouveau & Art Deco Jewelry, Baker	$9.95
1714	Black Collectibles, Gibbs	$19.95
1128	Bottle Pricing Guide, 3rd Ed., Cleveland	$7.95
3717	Christmas Collectibles, 2nd Ed., Whitmyer	$24.95
1752	Christmas Ornaments, Johnston	$19.95
3718	Collectible Aluminum, Grist	$16.95
2132	Collector's Ency. of American Furniture, Vol. I, Swedberg	$24.95
2271	Collector's Ency. of American Furniture, Vol. II, Swedberg	$24.95
3720	Coll. Ency. of American Furniture, Vol III, Swedberg	$24.95
3722	Coll. Ency. of Compacts, Carryalls & Face Powder Boxes, Mueller	$24.95
2018	Collector's Ency. of Granite Ware, Greguire	$24.95
3430	Coll. Ency. of Granite Ware, Book 2, Greguire	$24.95
1441	Collector's Guide to Post Cards, Wood	$9.95
2276	Decoys, Kangas	$24.95
1629	Doorstops – Id. & Values, Bertoia	$9.95
1716	Fifty Years of Fashion Jewelry, Baker	$19.95
3817	Flea Market Trader, 9th Ed., Huxford	$12.95
3731	Florence's Standard Baseball Card Price Gd., 6th Ed.	$9.95
3819	General Store Collectibles, Wilson	$24.95
3436	Grist's Big Book of Marbles, Everett Grist	$19.95
2278	Grist's Machine Made & Contemporary Marbles	$9.95
1424	Hatpins & Hatpin Holders, Baker	$9.95
3884	Huxford's Collectible Advertising – Id. & Value Gd., 2nd Ed	$24.95
3820	Huxford's Old Book Value Guide, 6th Ed.	$19.95
3821	Huxford's Paperback Value Guide	$19.95
1181	100 Years of Collectible Jewelry, Baker	$9.95
2216	Kitchen Antiques – 1790 - 1940, McNerney	$14.95
3887	Modern Guns – Id. & Val. Gd., 10th Ed., Quertermous	$12.95
3734	Pocket Guide to Handguns, Quertermous	$9.95
3735	Pocket Guide to Rifles, Quertermous	$9.95
3736	Pocket Guide to Shotguns, Quertermous	$9.95
2026	Railroad Collectibles, 4th Ed., Baker	$14.95
1632	Salt & Pepper Shakers, Guarnaccia	$9.95
1888	Salt & Pepper Shakers II, Guarnaccia	$14.95
2220	Salt & Pepper Shakers III, Guarnaccia	$14.95
3443	Salt & Pepper Shakers IV, Guarnaccia	$18.95
3890	Schroeder's Antiques Price Guide, 13th Ed.	$12.95
2096	Silverplated Flatware, 4th Ed., Hagan	$14.95
2348	20th Century Fashionable Plastic Jewelry, Baker	$19.95
3828	Value Guide to Advertising Memorabilia, Summers	$18.95
3830	Vintage Vanity Bags & Purses, Gerson	$24.95

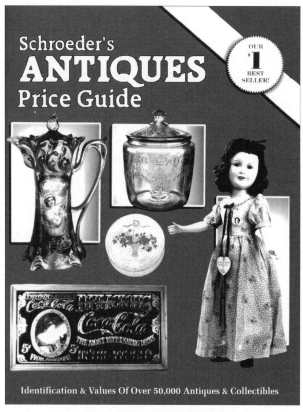